On Shady Lane

Marey -
I hope you
find a poem that
fits your pocket.
Christine

On Shady Lane

Poems by Christine McKee

Cherry Grove Collections

Published by Cherry Grove Collections
P.O. Box 541106
Cincinnati, OH 45254-1106

ISBN: 9781625491442
LCCN: 2015945299

Poetry Editor: Kevin Walzer
Business Editor: Lori Jareo

Visit us on the web at www.cherry-grove.com

Hugs and appreciation to Cecilia Caruso Zisk,
one half of Necki & Hokie, for the cover sketch.

Contact Christine McKee at: christine.mckee@verizon.net

Some of these poems, or some version of these poems,
have appeared in

And the Questions are Enough ~
Embroidery

Bucks County Writer ~
Some Day

Her Mark ~
Epitaph

L'Strange Café ~
*Family Album, What He Left Behind, Michael, This Easter There
Will Be No Babka*

Schuylkill Valley Journal ~
Breakfast Special

Survivor's Review ~
Waiting

U. S. 1 Poetry Anthology ~
Dressing Up

Thatchwork ~
Just to Clarify

Wood River Review ~
Where Are You Now

A tsunami of appreciation to Dr. Christopher Bursk
(poet, teacher, mentor),
gratitude to my parents Pasquale & Regina Caruso
(creative in so many ways),
Anthony F. Walsh
(primary cheerleader),
my siblings
(all eleven of them),
and the community of poets in Bucks County, PA.

Table of Contents

Part One

Just to Clarify	13
What's in a Name?	14
On Shady Lane	15
Life Lesson #1	17
Mea Culpa	18
High School Dance	19
Family Album	20
Michael	21
Finding Words	23
A Bottle Saved	24
Dressing Up	26
What Belonged to Her	27
Shame	29
The Sock	31

Part Two

Today's Breakfast Special	35
The Best Thing Before	36
Cooking Lesson	37
How to Select a Philly Soft Pretzel	39
Produce	40
This Easter There Will Be No Babka	41
Waiting	47
Where I Belong	48
Invitation to a Poet	49
Correction	50
Life Lesson #2	51
Excuses, Excuses	52
Embroidery	54
Leave Me a Poem	55

Part Three

Some Day	59
As if …	60
The Charms of the Ancient Mariner	61
Life Lesson #3	62
Where Are You Now?	63
Among the Threads	64
Decline	65
In His Mind's Eye	66
What He Left Behind	67
After the Last Day	68
The Night of Living Dangerously	69
Revenge of the Bangs	70
Towels	72
My Mother, the Car	73
Someday, Silence	74
She Will Wake to Find Her Own Mother	75
Epitaph	76
Untitled	77
As Winter Comes	79

Part Four

When You Grow Up	83
Distortions	84
Jesus Looked Back	85
Half-way to Heaven	86
Grief Comes to Call	87
Evolution	88

Part One

Just to Clarify

I've been wondering …

When you used to say
I wasn't worth a fiddler's fart,
did you mean somebody
like Seamus McCormack –
who wasn't opposed to having a nip before joining
Paddy Killoran and Jimmy Power
at the *Repeal of the Union* pub
on Saturday nights as they played their jigs and reels
or
were classical ones like Jascha Heifetz,
named the Violinist of the Century,
or Itzhak Perlman, child prodigy
featured on the Ed Sullivan Show at age 13
included in your reference?

It could make a difference.

What's in a Name?

My name is Christine.
Chr-chr-chr…too difficult for toddlers to say
who found Tris an easy substitute.

Add a "t" said too fast and hard ~
a near curse ~ demerits and a teacher saying,
"I know what you meant!"

But add the "ine" and draw it out ~
fine crystal tapped with a knife,
the crack of ice under boots on a January morning ~
both syllables with equal force, fairness,
enough for both to share without stinting.

On Shady Lane

In his black-and-white world,
Ward chatted amicably as he helped June to wash
the dinner dishes in their immaculate kitchen.

In my technicolored universe,
my sisters and I rotated jobs each week,
setting and clearing the dinner table
washing the dishes for ten, twelve, fourteen people
drying and putting them away
and joined together to fold laundry.

Mrs. Cleaver, in shirtwaist dress and pearls,
made housekeeping look effortless and
served home-baked cookies
with tall glasses of milk to Wally and the Beav.

On shopping trips to the Rising Sun Avenue A&P
while my father went to the meat counter,
my mother would hold the cellophane wrapped package
of Ann Page cookies, count the number enclosed
and then divide by the number of children,
figuring that we could each get two of the large oatmeal cookies
or three of the small coconut for our school lunches.

The Cleavers never seemed to have money problems
on their grassy, flowered, quarter-acre lot,
a bicycle for each boy, and furniture that matched.

My mother wrote on 5x8 index cards: Date, $ in, $ out, Total,
designated their use: food, electric, gas, telephone, shoes ...

and then folded and taped them to hold the few bills
that would be inserted each week once the
careful, budgetary calculations had been made,
every expenditure a decision and the occasional penny
for candy at the store six-blocks away ~
malt balls, maryjanes, caramel swirls ~
a cause for celebration.

Mrs. Cleaver made each of the boys' lunches separately,
with enough mayo to cover the whole surface of the bread
even to the edges, added fruit, snacks, and a napkin.

At my house, we placed the full loaf of thin-sliced bread
on the table in rows and columns, like dealing cards,
one slice of baloney on bread in the first, third, and fifth columns
and a slice of bland, American cheese on each of the others.
After a swipe of mustard, we flipped the two halves into a whole,
wrapped them in wax paper, replaced them in the bread bag,
and put them all in the freezer until ready to be grabbed
and inserted into a well-worn, brown paper bag
along with the two-or-three pre-counted, pre-wrapped cookies.

At 211 Pine Street, the Cleavers gathered for dinner each night.

At 205 Shady Lane, the fourteen Carusos did, too.

Life Lesson #1

First,
they gave me instructions
like cryptograms.

Then,
eyes covered,
body spun,
ears bombarded with shouts and jeers,
I was shoved forward,
flailing arms, hands out-stretched,
baby steps and banged-up knees.

Even now,
rushing frantically forward,
mistakes and missteps,
I still seek the right donkey
on which to pin the tail.

Mea Culpa

Mea culpa
I had trouble learning to read,
the letters clothed in sheepskin
changed their sounds,
left me clueless to their true identities.

Mea culpa
for a brain that froze numbers
and then tossed them turvsy-topsy
like snowflakes in a whiteout
that blurred my thinking.

Mea culpa
for not knowing which note was higher in pitch
as they floated amid my daydreams
and rested somewhere between
Nancy Drew and Rocky the Squirrel.

Mea culpa
for my mousy hair, eyes that bulge,
crooked teeth, nondescript self.

Mea culpa
for being another mouth to feed
more laundry to fold,
more cause for worry.

Mea culpa,
mea maxima culpa.

High School Dance

What were they thinking -
those parents who chaperoned high school dances
held in the basement of the local church -
when they would glide across the floor
looking for couples who were having a too-good time
then tap them on the shoulder and say,
"That's enough of that."

Did they think that, left unattended,
he or she,
might throw the partner to the floor in a fit of passion,
rend the clothes from the prostrate lover,
and, having been driven wild by the thought of sweet hard sex
teach the rest of us a how-to lesson?

Ah, we innocents should have been so lucky.

Family Album

~ for my father

Trying to capture the past
even as it cascaded through your fingers,
I asked each member of the family to write a memory.

I helped you with yours
after you forgot you had a son
and repeated your words
not knowing that you were repeating your words,
no longer knowing how to capture your thoughts.

Later I asked, *How about doing the dedication?*
You took the pen like an alien tool,
stared at it, and then at the paper.

You, who had written short stories
and who had read all the classics,
looked with eyes that questioned,
trying to make sense of my words.
Then, a moment of clarity. After writing,
"I will always love all of you, Dad."
you dropped your head into your hands
and wept.

Michael

I.

In the ethereal space between then and now -
in your place of shadow and stone -
I beseech you … What was the last
thoughtpicturememoryideaemotion
that went through your mind as you sat,
back propped against the pillows
in that ramshackled motel room
with the gun you stole
pressed against your head
finger squeezing the trigger
a nanosecond before the bullet
pierced your skull,
exploded your brain,
splattered blood,
and ended the you
we still miss today?

II.

Did you know that it would be
a minimum wage grandmother
working to supplement social security
who didn't mind making beds and cleaning toilets
but who had never really become accustomed
to the rooms that had been trashed,
who found you
body intact but head blown away
on that day before Thanksgiving?

III.

They,
mother with daughter and remaining son,
stand
not with their eyes toward heaven
but cast down
arms over shoulders
around waist
as they look upon the youngest,
head filled with plaster to hide the hole
face painted over to disguise sudden death
and lips giving no reason why.

IV.

Ashes in a golden vessel
next to your high school graduation picture
atop the entertainment center.
You have no final resting place
unless you consider the stone
that forever presses against her heart.

V.

Even now, five years later,
she still presses your sweatshirt -
the one with your dropped-out college name
found in the back of a closet -
close to her face
seeking one final scent.

Finding Words

 My mother used to study languages just for fun,
corrected our grammar, and that of everyone on TV.
Not seen but have seen!
Sitting around the dining room table after dinner
doing homework with my brothers and sisters,
I'd sometimes ask her for the spelling of a word
that I wanted to use to show-off for my teacher,
only to be told to sound it out or look it up in the dictionary.
But in a language where *good* and *food*
look like they should rhyme but don't,
where *night* and *neighbor* have stealth letters
like alligators in a moat …
her refusal seemed unreasonable and,
too lazy to plumb the depths of the dictionary,
I selected less beguiling words
for my third grade spelling sentences.

I began to wonder if Carolyn Keene was in on the conspiracy
when Nancy Drew novels inserted words such as
inveigle or *confederates* amid the ordinary prose,
like fine English porcelain on the same shelf as tin plates.

Reader's Digests were ever so innocently placed around the house
with *Increasing Your Word Power* challenging me
to select the correct definition among four offered.
I would study the twenty words and commit them to memory.

As a teacher, I encouraged my students
to think of the dictionary as a map leading to a treasure
of golden words that would enrich their lives.

Now, if only I could place those marvelous words into poems.

A Bottle Saved

~ for Dennis and Ceily

My brother was skinny back then but,
with that red hair, stood out among the caddies
waiting to carry a golf bag or two.
Doctors were the worst tippers he used to tell us
and the caddy master took his cut. Still
there was enough to buy a bottle of Gruber's soda
from Hoffmeier's store on the pike.
I begged to have the empty bottle so I
could trade it in for the two-cent deposit
and buy some orange slices, b-b-bats, candy buttons.

My brother gave it to me but it was too late
to go to the candy store and I put the empty aside.
Next day, same thing and it dawned on me
that, if I waited until I had seven empties,
I could buy my own soda.

It was two weeks before I had seven bottles,
six to cover the cost and one for the two-cent deposit …
a never-ending cycle of commerce.

When I had enough bottles, I had to decide which flavor.
What started as an obvious choice, expanded into possibilities
suggested by my sister who promised to help me
carry the bottles in exchange for a swig or two.

Cream, black-cherry, grape, orange.
We debated the merits of each.

Up Jarrett Avenue, orange with its sweet tang was number one.
Making a right onto Abington, grape was gaining ground.
Left on Sylvania and the thoughts of black-cherry
tickled my tongue. By the time we crossed the pike,
we had decided.

As the bottles clanged onto the counter,
Ceily spotted a sign on the ice cream case.
Chocolate-covered vanilla ice cream on a stick
cost seven cents. I bought two.

Dressing Up

with gratitude to Isabel

Twelve years of wearing school uniforms
did not diminish my sister's interest in fashion.
Well past the junior prom
(a forest green dress with a tulle-flared skirt)
and the hippie era (peasant garb with a loose fitting blouse),
Gina glommed onto the latest trends.
When pantsuits were introduced, she was there to make friends
with the tailored slacks, silk shells, and fitted jackets.
Performing her cabaret act in New York City,
she carefully orchestrated the songs,
the patter between, and her wardrobe.

More recently she was a devotee of black
to match her salt-and-pepper hair with a splashy scarf
faux-carelessly arranged. That's what she was wearing
when she stepped off the curb to cross the street,
and was struck by the cyclist,
the back of her head slamming
against the cobblestone curb,
till her brain shifted violently.

Four and a half years later, my younger sister Isabel,
honoring Gina's penchant, removed the flannel nightgown
while her body was still flaccid and replaced it
with maroon trousers, a winter-white sweater, a dab of lipstick,
dressing her up one last time.

What Belonged to Her

for Ceily

None of the new shoes my mother brought home
from Lit Brothers bargain basement
were the right size my younger sister, Ceily.
She was given the oxblood saddle-shoes
that had belonged to an older sister,
disappointed until she noted the color matched her hair.
They rattled on her feet as slick laces
made them hard to keep tied.
Close enough my mother said
wear an extra pair of socks until your feet grow.

But socks were another problem,
having been passed down from sister to sister
and never enough clean pairs to go around.
Ceily picked a dingy one and then another off the floor.
Already stretched beyond their limits,
they hung loosely around her ankles.
Halfway to school, they were in her shoes
having slipped with each step,
now cocoons around her feet.

Even our dresses had belonged to older sisters,
red and black plaid with a once-white bib and ribbon,
had already been worn to school that week.
Her red hair and blue eyes were handed down, too,
from our second-generation Irish grandmother but,
at recess that day, as she stood on the edge of the asphalt,
pawing the ground with one foot,
getting ready to charge down the hill,

Ceily knew with certainty that everyone
saw her just as she saw herself:
a beautiful, powerful, speeding filly,
with a mane and tail flying in the wind
that belonged to her and her alone.

Shame

In elementary school, I could never understand
why people always asked the same dumb questions
-       *Do you know all their names?*
-       *Do you have a washing machine?*
-       *Do you eat in shifts?*
when they learned I had lots of sisters and a couple of brothers.

It was my third grade teacher who made it clear
that something was terribly wrong with my family when,
after telling her my mother had a baby girl,
she replied *Some people don't know when to stop.*
What could I do but slink back to my desk
and spend the rest of the day with a tummy ache that
neither lunch nor recess could make better.

It was a longer walk home that February afternoon,
knee socks loose around ankles, and a hat left in the cloakroom
because Betsy had swung it around her head with one hand,
held her nose with the other, and asked in a loud cackle
who it belonged to before tossing it on the floor.
I could not admit the hat was mine.

Ears ringing with cold, nose nothing more than a faucet,
eyes streaming into a gooey mess amassing on my face,
I smeared it on my coat sleeves, first one than the other.
I ran to catch up to my siblings waiting at the corner.
The crossing guard pulled a tissue from a pack,
told me to hold still and gently dabbed my face.

Vincent took my school bag and flung it over his shoulder,
Suzanne wrapped her scarf around my head,
and the crossing guard, asking if I could be her assistant,
gave me the stop-sign to hold while motorists waited
in their warm cars for walkers to cross the street.

Arriving home, I went to look at my newest sister
asleep in her crib by the piano. Blankets to her neck,
head to one side, lips pursed in a prospective kiss.

Why did I still feel shame?

The Sock

I, too, lost the occasional sock in the dryer
sure it would emerge from the folds of a fitted-sheet
or clinging to a sweater. Such was my confidence;
I fretted little over its absence.

Suggestions by my older sisters that socks were removed
from the dryer by gremlins, melded with other ingredients ~
dragonfly wing, hoof of a gazelle,
a snippet of wind on a blustery day ~
to complete a spell of unknown virtues,
were scorned by my less-fanciful self. But –
how to explain this errant sock - a child's to be sure,
silvery-gray with embroidered sports decals,
amid my Memory Walk tee-shirt, underwear, and jeans
being removed from my dryer?

Was it misdirected to my house by astral projection gone awry,
leaving a child somewhere with only one warm foot,
his grandmother scolding *But it must be somewhere!*

Or, dropped by an elf sent to return it to its rightful owner
with only trace elements of magic clinging to the fibers
who is now having his ears boxed for the misdirection?

Or, could this sock be a reminder all these years later
that a child could have lived here,
should have lived here,
might have lived here,
if only,

if only,
I had had the courage.

Part Two

Today's Breakfast Special

"Two eggs
laid this very morning
just as the sun was rising over the rich green meadow
laced with the remnants of dew
by hens whose diet of organically grown corn
produced thick breasts and meaty legs
that kept their eggs warm
until our PhD educated farmhands,
wearing 400-thread Egyptian cotton gloves
eased them every so gently from their moorings
while Schubert's Symphony No. 8 in B minor
placed them in the Zen of life
and coddled them into our kitchen
ready to be cracked on our granite counter-top and
~ your choice ~
whipped into a frenzy
or laid bare in the pan."

"Do you have time to hear about the toast?"

The Best Thing Before

"Acorns were good until bread was found."
Francis Bacon

How could we ever have imagined that acorns –
gathered by children and old women
now too weak to work the fields
but still strong enough to stoop or reach -
were cracked, smashed, dried,
ground into bits like moist sand
then mixed with water, seeds, and,
maybe if they were lucky, honey
from a nearby hive, then
molded together into the shape of smooth stones,
of hands pressed in prayer,
and placed near the fire to bake into dense loaves,
taken to the fields for the noon-day meal,
grabbed and gobbled by the children –
could ever have been considered

the best thing before sliced bread?

Cooking Lessons

On the table before her, a dozen eggs
to be separated and beaten like pairs of illicit lovers.
Romeo and Juliets, cracked, divided,
once inseparable beings now into separate bowls,
ten times without mercy and then
the last two allowed to remain together
hope-against-hope until they, too,
are added to the yolks and whipped
into a frenzied, frothy, excited golden pool.

Add a tablespoon of melted butter
three Ts of sugar and cognac
and one each of orange and vanilla extracts,
one each of grated orange and lemon rind,
half as much salt.
Is the cup of sour cream half-empty or half-full?
No matter now completely blended with
four, perhaps five, cups of flour,
and stirred until fairly stiff.

It needs to be kneaded, (who doesn't), so what's stopping you,
ooh, feels good, right there, you know how I like it.
Keep it up for eight-or-ten minutes and then
place the dough on the counter, take the rolling pin –
long, hard but easily handled –
push, and press, and spread it thin.

Slash into strips, three inches by two, see if I care …
acrobatics as you slit each in the middle and pull one end through.

Now tied into knots, dip in the hot tub of lard and crisco –
but just for a minute – before drained on a paper towel,
exhausted, all done in, and ready to be powdered.

The egg whites?
Darling, they can wait until morning.

How to Select a Philly Soft Pretzel

First,
find the vendor at 8th and Market Streets -
the one who pisses into a McDonald's cup
when he thinks no one is looking
or those who do won't care -
the same one who hacks up TB phlegm into his hand,
rubs it onto his ratty, stained pants
before reaching for your pretzel.

Second,
make sure the pretzels have been fumigated
by the rancid exhaust from SEPTA buses,
delivery trucks, and cars with broken mufflers.

Third,
should you be given the opportunity,
select the pretzel with the fewest roach eggs,
ask to have it be put in one of the bags
that hadn't fallen to the sidewalk
where shoe scrum, blackened gum,
and spit from man and beast was ground into it.

Fourth,
squirt yellow, sharp-tasting mustard from the container
with caked and crusted remnants of god-knows-what around the
rim
onto your bready treat before indulging because -
New York can have its cheesecake,
and New Orleans its jambalaya -
but this is the one and only,
genuinely authentic Philadelphia delicacy.

Produce

So many from which to choose …

I select a black-skinned plum,
cradle it in my hands
roll it back-and-forth,
        one hand to the other
a juggler warming up,
readying herself for what comes next.

I feel the weight, the round, taut firmness,
run my finger along its river valley,
where two halves became a whole.

Yes, this is the one
to place at the end of the line
and to declare the poem complete.

This Easter There Will Be No Babka

A friend is someone who knows you
and loves you just the same.

Elbert Hubbard

I.

Maybe if I had browned the beef first,
sautéed the onions to a translucent yellow,
selected only organic vegetables,
washed them with more care,
cut them with greater precision,
seasoned them with herbs,
and used home-made broth.

If only I had pureed the stew
into a finer mix,
fed it to you in smaller sips
allowing it to wallow in your mouth
before urging you to swallow.

II.

Your hair vanishing and then, presto,
returned looking like someone else's
ditto times three.

You became lighter than air
with bird bones sticking through clothes,
morphine the only food you could keep down
and then what kept you down
for the final count.

41

III.

I sat across from you amid the wires and tubes,
your eyes at half-mast, lids flickering,
voice a raspy whisper ~ nail on an emery board ~
and listened again to your question.

You needed assurance that we would meet
in that perfect world that awaited believers,
born or reborn, to your belief of life and death
and life again.

To comfort you more than the morphine drip
ever could, I lied. I let you believe
that our thirty-seven years of friendship
would continue over this hurdle just as it had
when I didn't like your choice of boyfriends,
your decision to drop out of college,
or my own idiosyncrasies.

But did I do you, or your family, a favor?
With all concerns resolved, farewells completed,
you had something better to die for and so,
went to wait for others who would surely follow
and to discover that I would not be among them.

IV.

Even when it took four years
eight operations
sixteen drugs
thirty-two trips to doctors

sixty-four chemos
one-hundred-twenty-eight radiations
and the growing awareness that your prayers
would be answered His way,
you continued to believe.

V.

I sat at your kitchen table
on that bright, brisk morning you died -
right there where you and I shared pots of tea
and homemade babka -
and asked your husband,
"Is there anything I can do?"

He looked at me with purple, frozen eyes,
a cold, damp sheen on his face,
hands only slightly quivering and,
with a staccato voice,
concentrating on each and every syllable,
answered.

You died just in time
for me to be sent
to cancel his Christmas gift to you -
a heart-shaped necklace -
he had put on layaway.

VI.

Recognizing but not speaking the truth,
when you could still drive alone to the mall,

you bought small gifts that summer –
perfume for Lauren,
a CD for Mike,
and a game cartridge for Joe -
wrapped them in last year's leftover paper,
the one with snowmen holding candy-canes,
and hid them
--- how I'll never know in a house so small ---
so the they would be ready to be placed under the tree.

When you slipped away on Christmas Eve morning
morphine easing your passage,
your husband read your note,
found the gifts and placed them,
as you had each year before,
next to the crèche.

VII.

Later,
after we walked away from your new home,
in a neighborhood lined with
named and numbered granite slabs,
stone ornaments, and trees spaced among the rows,
whenever I would shut my eyes,
I'd see the earth around you
sliced open, cutting through the box,
and exposing you in your shrouded sleep.

VIII.

With the coming of spring we'd start our yearly journey,
a pilgrimage to Kensington to the Baltic Bakery –

not much more than a storefront on East Allegheny Avenue.
I coveted the babka with thick cords of soft, sweet cheese
woven within cakey flesh.

For your mother and grandmother, you selected one with poppies
and for your husband and children, plain and another with raisins,
sacramental breads to grace your Easter table.

We bought extra to enjoy that day -
thick slices blessed with butter, tea, and conversation.

Why did it take me three years to realize that it wasn't just you
whose life had been ended, but the one we shared for so many
years,
with its common, ordinary acts?

IX.

For decades
you lived your fantasy life through my adventures.
I envied you your family and home,
but not too much.

Then, Cancer came into the room,
catching us by surprise,
first forcing you onto the dance floor
for a long, slow number.

Then, that sly dog flirted with me, too.
Cozying up at the bar, cigarette
an exclamation point in his smile,
he offered to show me the two-step.

Finally, he chose you as his new best friend,
to have and to hold until death did you part.

And I was left to find my own way home.

Waiting

They numbed my eyes
before probing them with brilliant lights.
They forced the lids to remain open
while trying to capture the tumor on film.
They encircled my eye in a pool of gel
to compute its dimensions.
Doctors, lots of doctors.
And now, in this darkened room
just me, alone, waiting.

I ignore:
the cincture tightening around my head
the ice pick piercing my throat
the steel bands crushing my chest
the block of ice encasing my legs.

Muffled voices and footsteps
pass outside the door.

I'm waiting ever so calmly
because I refuse to think about
losing my sight,
telling my Mom,
having my lover say,
Hasta la vista, Baby!

Where I Belong

I surrendered to the pull on my body,
some magnetic force drawing me
past the cocktail language, coifed
hair, Capri pants and Stuart Weitzman sandals,
through the Widdicomb chaise of flowered damask
beyond the brown and gold striped brocade wallpaper
between the particles of drywall
and into the space that separates
the here-and-now
from the there-and-then.

Spider webs with mummy flies,
remnants of the builders –
an empty bottle of Piels with a blanket of dust
resting like a soldier against the stud,
a crumpled pack of Camels,
a paper sack with *Joe* scribbled in pencil

Here in the solitude, my forehead against the lathing,
cacophony muted, at last I can exhale.
If only I could remain always inside these walls
to glide unseen between rooms - a forgotten guest -
untouched by daily woes, and
nestled in my utopian world.

Invitation to a Poet

~ for David S. Berg

Stir the bottom of your ocean,
release the silt of fragmented dreams,
suppressed desires, ambivalent lusts
that once inhabited the dark, crushing depths,
and cajole them toward the light,
past the sea pen and squid,
holding tight to the tail of the lantern fish,
rising ever so carefully
like a scuba diver avoiding the bends,
and bring them to the surface,
to be washed, gutted, dried,
and displayed among the cockle shells
and driftwood on the beach:
      a rainbow of worries,
      a kaleidoscope of fears,
      a treasure trove of desires.

Correction

In the obituary for Justin Case,
we should have printed
his mother's name as Emma Pickett,
owner of the Invisible Fence Company.
Mr. Case was president of the
Emergency Alert Systems on W. Park Avenue
not Secure-it 4U on E. Main Street.
The correct names of his children are
Bree, Attashay, and May-cup,
so named in memory of Mr. Case's fraternal grandmother,
not his maternal grandfather.
He was a member of the Fraternal Order of Eagles
(which combats juvenile delinquency)
not the Fraternal Order of Beagles
(which fights negative stereotypes
as portrayed in comic strips).
Burial arrangements were under the direction of the
Happy Trails Funeral Home
not the Happy Tails Grooming House.

The editors sincerely regret any distress
these errors may have caused.

Life Lesson #2

Even those children
whose mothers stay
are sometimes still abandoned.

Excuses, Excuses

Can't find a way to explain why you didn't write
that poem you had a week to finish?
Caught without a plausible lie in your back pocket?
I'm here to rescue you.

Keep it simple. Easier to remember, easier to believe.

Not that the dog ate your homework but
your younger brother, that little rascal, crumpled it,
shoved it *and* his fist in his mouth, chewed and chomped.
Now a soggy mass, ink smeared, too many germs
since he also has a very messy cold.

Not that you left it in your locker but
your sister put your only copy through the shredder
because you wouldn't give her the TV remote.

Never because you forgot,
(after all it was an important assignment to you, too!)
but you worked late into the night, time got away,
you woke to find your face dented by your pencils,
your mother shoving toast into your hand
as you ran to catch the bus.
Golly, your mom's a real champ.

Be ready to apologize with genuine sincerity,
express disappointment in yourself
(before your teacher has a chance)
or, if too late for that, agree with him wholeheartedly
as you hang your head, the burden of the shame
too much to bear. Refrain from rolling your eyes,

giggling, or doing a victory-dance until your teacher
is around the corner or has disappeared into the lounge.
His hope of your success must be maintained.
Scribble any sentences that come into your head,
break them into short lines, (sort of like this poem),
and hand it in the very next day expressing pride
at your own efforts, eager for his feedback and then …

try these techniques on your algebra teacher.

Embroidery

Take the needle
threaded with black strands
twisted into yarn,
puncture the cloth,
pierce the surface
then, just a thought away,
pull the needle beneath the cloth
held tight by the wooden ring,
make it taut while you remember
the smoky color of his eyes
on that last day,
wonder how it had all come to that.
Pause no longer than it takes
for the tea to cool,
and press the needle through
and back … again, again, again
until the line is formed across the borders.
Now that it is done,
drive the needle down,
sip the tea,
snip the thread,
tie a final knot
just below the surface.

Leave Me a Poem

I won't be long.
I'm only going to fill the kettle
and set it on the stove …
to fix a tray with scones and butter.
Or would you prefer jam?

I want to spend time with you
but I must check on the children,
to hear the pattern of their breathing,
to make sure the blankets are in place.

I'll only be a minute but,
just in case, listen for the whistle,
pour the water into the teapot,
and cover it with the cozy.

If you must go …
at least turn down the flame and
leave me a poem on my chair.

Part Three

Some Day
for Tony

Some day
when we aren't surrounded by gardening tools
and knee deep with annuals awaiting their new home,

or at the north rim of the Grand Canyon
in awe of the summer-lit vermilion walls,

or on the bridge over the canal in Venice
eavesdropping on the gondolier's serenade below,

or walking through autumn woods
and feeling as if we own them,

or laughing about the fun we had shoveling
that first crisp snow of the season,

or when we aren't at the hospital pre-op room
with your arm reassuringly placed over my shoulder,

maybe then,
I'll tell you how I really feel.

As if …

As if it were a challenge to love you now,
to spend time together, plan our future.
As if it weren't enough that you listen
to my stories, laugh at the right places,
now you explain football to my 87 year old demented mother
… downs … yardage … penalties … field goals …
and wave me away when I mouth, "What are you doing?"
You tell me to leave her alone, she's getting it,
even asking good questions. When you told her
you were rooting for the home team, she started the rosary,
wouldn't stop to talk to me until it was over and
the Eagles had won 30-10.

At dinner that night, you doted on her,
offered her a glass of wine, a buttered roll, and then,
as if you weren't quite satisfied,
rose from the head of the table,
carried the gravy boat to her place,
and gave her just as much she wanted.

The Charms of the Ancient Mariner

At the beginning of the encounter,
my head rests on your belly.
Sounds like mating whales,
the rhythmic tide of your breathing
lift me, a raft on water,
an ancient cadence now quickening,
my feathery kisses descending the curve of your hip,
your voice, soft with desire and danger,
implores me to take us to the netherworld.

Life Lesson #3

The other night, I remember thinking
but not saying, even as it was happening,
that these moments when we are sitting
around your kitchen table
with a cup of tea and conversation
will some day hold
an extraordinarily, exquisite beauty
when one of us is no longer.

Where Are You Now?

You sit near the window, arms slack, legs splayed,
head slightly bowed and tilting to the right,
flecks of skin gather above your brow,
whiskers highlighted by the sun,
short silver spikes casting no shadows,
eyes vacant.

I wipe the saliva from your chin,
lean closer, I want to memorize the feel
of my lips on your forehead,
my hand resting on your shoulder.

Where is the rest of you now?
on the golf course,
wet grass soaking your canvas shoes

in a six-footer out on the bay,
quietly drifting, waiting for a bite

in the driver's seat of the Ford wagon,
kids akimbo in the back, out for a Sunday ride

at the Fox Chase library,
selecting Hesse, Fowles, Thurber, Lardner

a paradise of possibilities

Among the Threads

Who can say what next will be?
Upon my loom my father laid the warp.
Will what happened to him happen to me?

My mother, using filaments with indelible designs,
shuttled them among the threads creating my form.
Who can say what next will be?

Well-worn in service to country and home
my father's tapestry was splayed in the setting sun.
Will what happened to him happen to me?

Colors once vibrant and sturdy began to fade,
the framework of our lives, slowly unraveled.
Who can say what next will be?

He, with fingers unable to grasp the folds,
slid into oblivion one hue at a time.
Will what happened to him happen to me?

What patterns imprinted within the fabric of my cloak
are secretly waiting to emerge?
Who can say what next will be?
Will what happened to him happen to me?

Decline

*~ Words my father might have written, had he been able,
to describe his experience with Alzheimer's Disease.*

I used to be able to think my thoughts but
that was before amyloid plaques
caused clumps of protein to coat
my brain's nerve cells,
before the tangles blocked the process
that stores and retrieves information.

Now, inside my head,
I can still hear my thoughts but
they are like bees buzzing over a field of clover
and I stand, net in hand, unable to capture them.

I can still see my thoughts
But they are like fireflies flitting
in the dusk of a summer night,
here, no there …

I can still feel my thoughts but
now they crawl along my skin
getting caught in the threads of my shirt.

I can no longer speak my thoughts.
I jangle the words like rocks in a tumbler.

If only I could ▲▶◀   ↓◀   △↓→↑◀   ⇨→⇨↓↔↘

In His Mind's Eye

It wasn't until later ~
when my mother's weeping subsided,
the hiccups ceased and the tissues,
filled with tears and phlegm,
were wadded into a ball and thrown away ~
that she was able to choke out the cause of her heartache.
And here was the reason:
Fifty years as husband-and-wife,
eking pennies from every dollar,
counting cookies in a pack to know
how many each child could have,
mending socks and uniforms,
mixing whole milk with skim to save money,
wallpapering every room,
righting a fallen Christmas tree,
attending children's concerts,
mowing the lawn,
planting a garden,
raking leaves,
shoveling snow,
the birth of nineteen grandchildren
and the death of one,
were not enough to enable my father
to rip through the amyloid plaques
that tangled his brain
and interfered with his recognition
of my mother's face when
smiling at me, he said
At last you're here.

What He Left Behind

A black leatherette jewelry box
with a lining red and torn. Inside
      black wooden and worn rosary beads
      57 cents in five coins
      a stone picked up at Normandy beach
      one stainless steel tie clip from the Budd Company
      a social security card with his chicken-scratch signature
      one watch stopped at 2:05
      a 1987 driver's license with eyes frozen open.

After the Last Day

The shards of glass in my stomach
remind me that home-made casseroles
are threatening to take over the refrigerator,
to instigate a revolt, demand to be eaten
or commit suicide by mold.

Caramel light seeping below the window shade,
is a tell-tale sign that I've managed to remain oblivious
through a day of phone calls and well wishers.
I can't listen to another platitude about
how happy memories will ease the pain,
or, more reminders that time heals.

I know that it also steals.
It took its often-used soft, pink eraser
and little-by-little eliminated my father's
ability to recognize family,
to communicate, to swallow.

After months of only nonsense syllables,
sitting with him one Christmas night
before returning to the nursing home,
I burst into painful, stress-filled tears.
As he stared into the black of the windshield,
he said the last words I ever heard him speak,
She's crying.

The Night of Living Dangerously

You'd think that sharing a second floor bedroom
with four sisters, I would have felt safe,
that nothing really bad could ever happen to me.
But on a wintry night when my parents
were enjoying a rare evening out,
I heard a noise against the closed window
where no tree branches could reach.
Coming through the blinds tilted to emit
enough light to keep the monsters under the bed:
the shadow of a ladder highlighted by the streetlamp.
Too frightened to move, almost too scared to breathe,
I tried to think what to do. Call the police?
The telephone was downstairs. Scream?
My voice was hiding somewhere in my throat.

Then the rapping on the glass, knuckles
against the frosted pane, a voice calling my name.
I pushed my head further into the pillow,
tried to squeeze my body through the mattress.
I could see the outline of a hat, shoulders,
and heard the voice, *Wake up. Open the door.*
I didn't want to be kidnapped. Maybe if I ignored him,
he'd try another house. At last, relief
as the man finally lowered himself on the ladder.

At breakfast, my mother told us they had been locked out,
and knowing I was a light sleeper, tried to waken me
but had to wait for my older brother
to arrive home from a date.
With a practiced look of innocence I said,
Sorry, Mom. I never heard a thing.

Revenge of the Bangs

Scissors in hand, I am poised
to snip my mother's silver-white bangs.
Her once thick, luxurious hair
is now thinning, her freckled scalp beginning
to show between the strands.
Cut just a little she says.

Suddenly, I have an opportunity
longed for by my 1950s self
after my mother, time and time again,
sat me upon a high stool,
open my dead-grandfather's barbering kit,
and cut my hair. The side that was once
a little too long, with a few clips, became too short.
The new too-long side would be made shorter
until I was about to have
the ugliest haircut in my elementary school.
Sit down and stop bawling, I can fix it.

Drawing from the top and sides,
combing more hair onto my face,
my mother tried to make amends
but succeeded in creating a hair-do
only a scarecrow could admire.
And then, inspiration:
Let's try a new look I saw in a magazine.
She dipped her comb in water,
drew it through my hair, straightening
the tangled mess above my eyebrows,
and snipped my bangs up-and-down and up-and-down.

70

The cool metal of the scissors crept across my forehead
as strands of hair dusted down my face.
All done she says and picked up a mirror to show me.

The only picture my eight-year-old eyes could see
looked like a kid in a wanted poster
or the "before" shot in a commercial
for a beauty parlor. I was shocked and knew
that kids would laugh when they saw my hair
cut on a curve above each eyebrow
and coming to a longer point above my nose.
My, soon-to-be famous, heart-shaped bangs.

But now, fifty years later, instead of revenge,
I take pity on my mother, knowing that, at my best,
I'm likely to cut her hair on a slant.
Gently I snip, clip, cut, having her hold the trashcan
under her chin to catch the bits of hair.
When finished, I turn her toward the mirror
and ask her what she thinks:
Okay she says *but could you try to make them even?*

Towels

"It's okay if you want to throw in the towel,"
my sister says. *"No one will blame you."*

I wonder, does she think I need her permission
to change my mind or is she urging me to surrender,
or admit that, once again, I have jumped in water
not knowing how deep or what is hidden beneath the surface.

She threw me those words as if they were a life preserver,
urging me to be pulled to safety,
stretched out on the cement apron of the pool,
given CPR, and brought back to my own life.

And yet, it occurs to me without pride, that
I am the life preserver. I have wrapped my arms
around my mother when she was flailing
in the murky depths of dementia
and pulled her into my home.

We are struggling still ~
she, to make sense of a life without memory
and me to help her find the way.

My Mother, the Car

I remember when the timing belt in my Chevette broke.
I had it towed, the engine lifted, and a new belt installed.
If only the same could be done for my mother.

On the days when her pistons are misfiring,
she asks me who my parents are,
tells me that the crumbs on her breakfast plate look like Hitler,
whimpers that the tree in my neighbor's yard frightens her.

On the days when her battery is fully charged,
her sense of humor delights me, she tells stories
about her mother, Atlantic City in the 1920s,
how she met my dad. Then, she hedges on dessert
because, at age 87, has to watch her figure.

On the days when her sparkplugs are clogged,
she scolds me for not telling her where we are going,
is frustrated she cannot picture her husband's face,
seems to get lost in her fastidiously-kept bedroom.

On the days when her tires are fully inflated,
she cheerfully attends the adult day care center,
speaks a few words of Spanish to one of the seniors,
offers to fold laundry or prepare lunch.

After tucking her in bed each night,
I wonder when her motor will run out of gas the final time
and … if I have a similar make and model engine.

Someday, Silence

I cringed at your incessant repetition of stories
begun again even before the previous telling was complete,
your need to be reminded of the day or where we were going,
the guided tours of the bedroom I prepared for you.
Asking me, *Who are your parents?*

I wanted to scream, bloody scream.
But, at those moments,
I remembered the night that you awoke in sobs
because you couldn't remember if your older sister,
whom we had visited that day, was alive or dead.
With my arm around your shoulder,
reassuring you that all was well, you said,
I don't know what I would do without you.

She Will Wake to Find Her Own Mother

One time she'll just go to sleep and not wake up
my sister said. *From your mouth to God's ear,*
I replied, *but not just yet.*

My mother sleeps on my couch,
head on an accent pillow, feet on a blue towel,
a blanket draped over her now-shrunken body,
curved like a shrimp or question mark.
Just as a child who wears herself out playing
will plop on the sofa exhausted,
she finds her eyes weighted.
The puff-puff-puff of final breaths,
lips now finished with their daily task,
her mouth in a soft o.

In those empty hours before dawn,
it will be her father who scoops her into his arms
as she is transformed into that girl of eighty-plus years ago.
Soft corkscrew curls amid pink ribbons,
white cotton pinafore, translucent skin,
her head against his chest, arms and legs slack,
as he carries her upstairs to her room,
and gently places her beneath the covers.

With the coming of light, she will wake
to find her own mother waiting
in the rocking chair, a cup of tea
on a side table, a smile on her face.

Epitaph

Who knows if the ballerina
really stops dancing
once the box is closed?

Untitled

for Christopher Bursk

I still seek poems while sleeping ...
body flat on the surface
of the collective unconscious,
resting like a raft on jello,
reaching below the surface
as far as my arm will go.
I bend, face submerged below
the tangerine and turquoise,
sight distorted by the light beams of stars
infiltrating the pool as they glide along the universe,
lose my balance and tumble turvsy-topsy,
slow motion, arms flailing, mouth open to silence,
surrendering to the forces that control this alien world,
and slowly come to rest on a sunken ledge,
noticing with interest that I can breathe
in this subterranean world
where ancient sea creatures with
the faces of the deceased swim by,
glancing but not stopping,
in-and-out of sea grasses
the colors chartreuse and fuchsia,
me, a mere curiosity.

Filmy doilies of thought pass by without purpose,
seemingly dissolve when touched,
then reunite beyond my grasp.
I ease off my ledge, drift to the spongy floor
and gather in my arms all the words and ideas I can hold,
store them in the folds of my nightgown,

and inch-by-inch allow myself
to be drawn to the surface
where I shake the silver krill from my hair,
and without benefit of lamplight,
scribble in my bedside notebook,
words begging to become poem.

As Winter Comes

Had I known that the nights
would become dark weeping women,
my bones, timbers cut to divide the pale,
my heart in a vice-grip …

I would have looked more closely
at the crocuses and bluebells,
drenched my canvas sneakers in the morning grass,
woken early to see dawn cascade down the valley.

I would have reveled in the bright new earth,
spun circles in the meadow
amid tall grass and wildflowers,
splashed in the coolness of the pond,
and held each sun-saturated day in wonder.

I would have inhaled more deeply
the gingersnap autumn air,
taken more notice of the forest,
its frenzy of gold and rust,
danced among the leaves
as they surrendered and spun to the earth,
and exalted with the streamers of clouds
furled above the ridge.

As it is, there is still time to contemplate the stark trees
as they reach for redemption, the frozen shards
of ice sparkling on the moon-lit meadow
and to acquiesce to what waits ahead.

Part Four

When You Grow Up

When you grow up, don't get married.
My mother used to tell us time and again
when we were just trying to grow up.
No one to talk to, not even with all those sisters,
no one ever talked about anything, so I didn't either.

When you grow up, don't get married.
If you do get married, don't have kids.
Even in elementary school I knew this much:
She meant me.

Don't have a child like you,
you'll be as sorry as I am now.
In high school, I understood it was
almost all of us, nine sisters and two brothers
that made her life, no life. Who could blame her?

Tacit learning being what it is, I followed
her command, rejected my first prospective
husband, married/divorced/annulled
a candidate I knew would not succeed,
planned my own failure to prove her right.

Made sure I bore no children,
such was my need to please her,
to earn her approval.

Distortion

The same bug-eyes, round and protruding,
set too close together and placed within
soft pools of flesh are still there.

The once bushy eyebrows
my mother scolded me to brush up
so I'd avoid looking like a monkey.

Cheeks still scarred from acne,
a thin pointed nose above a mouth that
calls for fewer teeth, and folds in the skin

that form brackets from my nose
to arrowhead chin. Parentheses awaiting a quote.
I recall the front tooth broken in half in seventh grade

and never capped until I was out working.
What the mirror doesn't show were my efforts
to become invisible. More introverted

than older sisters and never as pretty
or effervescent, I made myself the dark contrast.
Muddled through years of night school,

refused to stop when people said I'd never finish,
never teach, never amount to anything.
An aunt my only cheerleader.

In the end, I was blessed.
Others peaked in high school.
I found self-acceptance and poetry.

Jesus Looked Back

My friend saw Jesus in her rearview mirror,
tapping his fingers on the steering wheel,
appearing to whistle a little ditty.
She wondered where he was going
and if she should follow.

I was at the VA Alzheimer ward
where my dad lived when He came to me.
So many veterans from the second war
now in geri-chairs, adult diapers, warm-up suits.
I looked for someone needing to be fed.
Mr. Nash, once a dashing private first class
waited, his dark pompadour and speech
long gone, grey sweats to match his hair,
hands and feet gnarled. Eyes cloudy.

I pulled a chair to his side, placed the over-size bib
across his chest, prepared the tray,
chatted about my job, my family.
I'd wait until he managed to thoroughly gum
the puree enough to swallow before
I moved the spoon back toward his mouth.

His blue eyes suddenly focused on mine,
became alert, bright, penetrating.
I recalled the comment Jesus made
Whatever you do to the least of my brethren,
that you do unto me. And, here He was to prove it.
I was looking at the eyes of Jesus, looking at me.
Fanciful? Perhaps.
But no one will convince me otherwise.

Half-way to Heaven

He wouldn't make it to the hospice unit
but we didn't know that then.
I had asked the nurse to have a fake I V
taped to my brother's arm, a theatrical prop,

so that my mom would think he was comfortable
as he lay slack in the hospital bed.
A surprise. He lifted his elbows off the bed.
My mother stroked his forehead
It's okay, Dennis, it's okay.

A few minutes later, the same motions
then still again. My mother kissed his forehead,
whispered a few words into his ear,
the final good-bye, although
she didn't know that then.

Other siblings and she left but
was I truly alone with my brother?
Dennis again lifted his arms but now also
his upper body and I envisioned my dead father
on one side and Dennis' deceased son on the other,
lifting, helping him out of the hospital bed.

When he rested back on the sheets,
I walked to his bedside,
It's okay Dennis, you can join them.
His eyes opened, brilliant blue,
his face that of a teen again, an almost smile,
staring past me, at something beyond.
Are they here, Dennis? Are they waiting for you?

When Grief Comes to Call

The unwanted guest stands on my porch,
dowdy top-hat perched above a monocle on a ribbon,
his coat worn thin, a calla lily on the lapel,
a mustache not more than a pencil line,
knocking on the door with staccato raps,
officious, calling through the screen, *I'm here.*

Too late to close the door on this September afternoon,
pretend I'm not in the house wearing sweats,
unwashed hair escaping the rubber band,
dry toast and a cup of coffee still on the table,
its coagulating cream staring back at me.
He presses the bell again and again,
chimes echoing in rooms.

Time has broken away from the rules of physics,
spun on itself. I try to push it back even further
to recall the last casual conversation,
wanting more, more mundane existence.
I stand absolutely still, squeeze my eyes,
silently chant *Go away - Go away - Go away.*

Alas, my refusal to respond re-doubles his efforts.
The authoritative voice like a despised teacher,
persistent, insistent calls *Shall I let myself in?*
I surrender and trudge through the living room.
You should have been expecting me.

Evolution

I stand by a stream from which
scales morphed into feathers
and fish became birds …
The longer I stand the more
I contemplate the intricate
mysteries of evolution.
I feel my own feet
becoming anchored to the soil,
my toes breaking through my soles,
entering the earth, growing down, down,
down to that deep pool beneath the earth's crust
that holds the collective unconscious …
secrets, dreams, the history of the world,
melding our experiences
with those who were and those who will be.

I notice that bark is encasing my legs,
inching up my torso, I fling my arms
toward the sky only to find they are boughs,
dozens of wispy branches with thin green leaves.
I toss what was once my head,
flail what were once my arms
and in that final second
before the change is complete,
I understand that I have been transformed
into a weeping willow
always to bend and rise,
to carry the sorrows
from the center of the earth
to the wind above the water,
and out to the universe.

CPSIA information can be obtained at www.ICGtesting.com
Printed in the USA
BVOW08s0901270715

410367BV00001B/2/P

9 781625 491442